DUDLEY

The Little Terrier That Could

by Stephen Green-Armytage

SCHOLASTIC INC.

New York Toronto London Auckland Sydney
Mexico City New Delhi Hong Kong

About Jack Russell Terriers

Often described as a big dog in a small body, the Jack Russell Terrier seems to be represented everywhere these days, from the PBS children's show *Wishbone,* starring a terrier who takes on different historical personas, to *Frasier,* featuring the enigmatic Eddie, to the indestructible Jack Russell on wheels in *Babe, Pig in the City,* to the magnificent athlete of the Mighty Dog dog-food commercials. Yet these enormously popular dogs have been around since the eighteenth century, when their compact size and talent for digging made them ideally suited for leading their hunter owners to underground animals such as foxes.

The Jack Russell Terrier was named after an English dog breeder, the Reverend John Russell, whose feisty personality apparently matched that of his dogs. This feistiness sometimes causes Jack Russells and other terriers to be misunderstood. Though intelligent, playful, and loyal, they do not always understand how to react gently to young children who don't yet know how to play gently with them, and they thrive with owners who can provide them with lots of space and time to work off their incredible energy.

ISBN 0-439-21881-0

Copyright © 1999 by Stephen Green-Armytage.
All rights reserved.
Published by Scholastic Inc., 555 Broadway, New York, NY 10012, by arrangement with Harry N. Abrams, Inc.
SCHOLASTIC and associated logos are trademarks and/or registered trademarks of Scholastic Inc.

12 11 10 9 8 7 6 5 4 3 2 1   0 1 2 3 4 5/0

Printed in the U.S.A.   24

First Scholastic printing, October 2000

Editor: Harriet Whelchel
Designer: Dana Sloan
Hand lettering: Tom Vanderschmidt

When Dudley was born, he was very, very small.

(He looked more like a mouse than a dog.)

His brother, Bentley (that's him on the right),

was the same size
(that's him on the left).

They were twins.

Dudley grew a little bigger, but children seemed like GIANTS,

whichever end of them he visited.

He was smaller
than your sneakers
    —yes, *your* sneakers.

He grew a little more,

but still he was small,

and other dogs
looked down on him.

And he grew a bit more,

but he was still small,

and BIG other dogs
really looked down on him.

By now Dudley knew that he would never be a LARGE dog,
but perhaps he could become an *ATHLETE* dog.

He could become fit, fast, and strong.

And so . . .

Dudley went into training!

He started weight lifting.

He trained in the winter and the spring,

and in the summer and the fall.

He went for long walks,
in the city and the country,

on hot summer days,

and in cold winter weather.

Dudley also went swimming,

but only on the hot summer days.

He loved to go running, in the winter and the summer,

with his friends and with his brother.

Every day, he did stretching exercises,

for the front end

and the back end.

He had plenty of rest, drank lots of water,

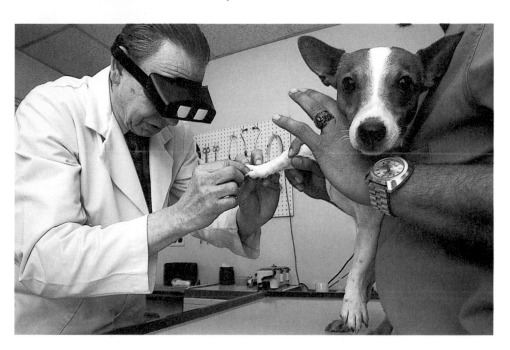

and went for his regular check-ups (as we all should do).

He learned to do chin-ups.

He did them in the winter and the spring

and (this will not surprise you)
in the summer and the fall.

By now Dudley was truly an *ATHLETE* dog.

All of a sudden (and this *will* surprise you),
he found that . . .

HE COULD FLY!

And so he did.

He soared through the air,

catching yellow Frisbees.

He sailed through the air,

catching yellow tennis balls

... most of the time.

Now Dudley could see that not all people were giants.

Sometimes he could even look down on them.

And sometimes they even needed his protection.

So was Dudley *really* any larger than before? Well, not exactly,
but now he was fit, fast, and strong, just as he had planned.

Now he has the muscles and the confidence and the smile
of a dog who DOESN'T EVEN CARE WHAT SIZE HE IS.

Now he can see that

it's the same big world for all of us.

Dedicated to the memory of Sydnor Vanderschmidt, who loved and admired Dudley and hoped that through this book more people would come to know this wonderful little dog.

Special thanks
to my wife, Judy, for bringing Dudley into our lives, for training him,
and for helping with many of the photographs;
George Soter, for his text suggestions;
and Kate McMullan and Peter Mayer, for their advice.